The Esse...

...conomic and Monetary Union (**EMU**) **will be
the system that links together the economies
and currencies of the participating European
countries. It will enter the third of its four
phases in January 1999 when:**

- exchange rates will be linked

- the euro becomes a currency in its own
  right and

- the European Central Bank becomes
  responsible for centralised monetary policy.

In July 2002 when EMU is complete:

- the euro will be the legal tender in the
  participating countries

- national currencies will be withdrawn

- the economies of the participating countries
  will run side-by-side inside of a single
  economic and monetary union.

What is EMU?

Economic and Monetary Union

means that all participating or "in"

countries of the European Union

will eventually share a common

monetary policy and a single

currency. This currency will be

called the euro and is due to take

full effect 1st July 2002.

What is EMU?

This will assist the European Union to become a more efficient single market in goods and services because they will be priced in the same currency. Buyers will be able to compare products and prices more easily and decide which to buy without having to take exchange rates into account.

EMU, which eventually may affect 15 countries and more than 350 million people, is to be phased in by stages. The process started in 1990. Apart from the logistics of producing and issuing notes and coins, changing over coin operated machines and a great many other practical steps that need to be taken, an entire new economic system needed to be established as a sound basis for monetary union.

This meant that the economies of the "in" countries had to match up - or largely match up - to certain key measures. By doing so they could adhere to the same currency, and use the same interest rates without causing strain to their economies within the EU. Bringing together the economies in this way is called "convergence".

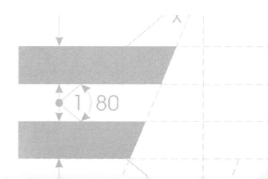

Convergence

The basis for convergence was set out in the Maastricht Treaty ratified in December 1991. The measures set out in the treaty are the Maastricht Criteria: see table opposite.

As at 3rd May 1998, 11 EU countries had sufficiently reached the criteria or were expected to have reached them in time for the next stage of EMU.

These so-called "in" countries were:

- Austria

- Belgium

- Finland

- France

- Germany

- Ireland

- Italy

- Luxembourg

- Netherlands

- Portugal

- Spain

Denmark, Greece, Sweden and the UK did not sign up for the first round of EMU at this time.

The Maastricht criteria

Price Stability	Average price inflation must be no more than 1.5% above that of "at most, the three best performing Member States in terms of price stability."
Sustainable government finances	• The ratio of general government annual deficit to GDP should be 3%.
	• The ratio of government debt to GDP should be no greater than 60%.
Interest rates	The average long-term interest rate should be no more than 2% above "that of, at most, the three best performing Member States in terms of price stability".
Exchange rate stability	Participation in EMS "within normal margins of fluctuation" for at least two years without devaluing.

When will the UK join?

1999

The short answer to this is "don't know".

However, the Chancellor of the Exchequer Gordon Brown in his 10th November speech to the Confederation of British Industry said that if it is "... good for business, jobs and prosperity...then Britain should join... We are in principle in favour of joining a successful single currency."

Various commentators have suggested that it is likely that the UK might well join if the Labour government remains in power for a second five-year term. This would result in the following theoretical timetable, but it is possible that the UK could join earlier or later than this or maybe not at all:

Possible Timetable for the UK to become part of EMU

October 2002	UK announces formal commitment to join EMU.
April 2003	Sterling irrevocably fixed against euro.
February 2004	Euro notes and coins become legal tender.
April 2004	Sterling ceases to be legal tender.

Timetable

The process of Monetary Union has been continuing since July 1990 in three stages. The timetable for participating "in" countries is as follows:

STAGE 1	STAGE 2	
	Phase A	
July 1990 - December 1993	**January 1994 – December 1998**	
Co-ordination of economic policies	Adoption of legal and administrative framework for conversion	Decision as to participating countries
Liberalisation of capital markets	Establishment of the European Monetary Institute	Establishment of the European Central Bank (ECB)

STAGE 3	
Phase B	**Phase C**
January 1999	**January 2002 - July 2002**
Irrevocable fixing of exchange rates for participating currencies and the Euro	Euro notes and coin are introduced as legal tender
Euro becomes a currency in its own right and replaces the ECU at a rate of 1:1	National currency notes and coins withdrawn
Introduction of euro for non-cash transactions	Changeover of public sector operations to euro is completed
ECB adopts responsibility for centralised monetary policy	Any outstanding public debt still denominated in national currency is redeemable only in euro

Courtesy of: National Westminster Bank Plc / The Hundred Group of Finance Directors

The Impact of the Euro on the markets

Money markets

The immediate effect of the beginning of stage three of EMU in January 1999 will be that ECB will manage the euro-denominated money market. This will cover all of the "in" countries and ECB will work with the central banks of the "in" countries.

Being an "out", the UK will continue with the Sterling money market.

Currency markets

The currencies of the 11 participating member states will effectively disappear (see timetable above). In the meantime, foreign exchange trading in those so-called "legacy currencies" will virtually disappear.

	100 B.Fr/Lux	100 Fr.Fr	100 D.M	1 Irish Pt	100 Gldr
Belg/Lux	–	614.977	2062.55	51.2210	1830.55
France	16.2608	–	335.386	8.32893	297.661
Germany	4.84837	29.8164	–	2.48338	88.7517
Ireland	1.95232	12.0063	40.2678	–	35.7382
Netherlands	5.46285	33.5953	112.674	2.79812	–
Portugal	496.984	3056.34	10250.5	254.560	9097.53
Spain	412.462	2536.54	8507.22	211.267	7550.30
Austria	34.1108	209.774	703.552	17.4719	624.415
Finland	14.7391	90.6420	304.001	7.54951	269.806
Italy	4799.90	29518.3	99000.2	2458.56	87864.4

At present however, with the exception of the Deutschemark, foreign exchange turnover in the legacy currencies is relatively small in global terms. Trading is dominated by transactions involving the US Dollar.

Following the formal launch of EMU on 1st January 1999, trading in euros will gradually increase. It is expected that eventually the euro will become a reserve currency playing a major role in world trade and currency trading.

As far as trades involving Sterling are concerned, we can expect to see those involving legacy currencies decrease, to be replaced by those involving Sterling-euro: *see table below*.

100 Escudo	100 Peseta	100 Schilng	100 Markka	1000 Lira
20.1214	24.2447	293.162	678.568	20.8338
3.27189	3.94237	47.6704	110.324	3.38773
0.975559	1.17547	14.2136	32.8947	1.01010
0.392834	0.473335	5.72347	13.2459	0.406743
1.09920	1.32445	16.0150	37.0637	1.13812
–	120.492	1456.97	3371.88	103.541
82.9929	–	1209.18	2798.42	85.9313
6.86357	8.27006	–	231.431	7.10657
2.96571	3.57345	43.2094	–	3.07071
965.805	1163.72	14071.5	32565.8	–

Equities

A number of developments are expected to happen during and after the transition to the single currency:

- An increasing number of companies will account and issue stock in euros

- Unified accounting standards, probably based upon American ones will become more prevalent

- European governments will issue less debt such as government bonds, or "gilts" in the UK, in order that they maintain their required level of public indebtedness

- More publicly owned companies across Europe will be privatised and their stock floated on one or more of Europe's stock exchanges. This will increase the total amount of equity stock in issue

- It will become easier to compare companies' performances and to make equity investment decisions

- A number of the European stock exchanges may merge perhaps into a single pan-European electronic stock market.

One very important development that is expected to happen is that investment in equities will become much more widespread throughout Europe, both as a result of all of these factors, but also because of the expected growth in private pension funds.

Bonds

- Effectively the market in euro denominated bonds has already begun

- Issuers have taken one of two routes: Either they are issuing in ECU which will convert on a 1:1 basis to euro, or they are issuing in so-called "tributary" or legacy currencies which will be easily convertible to Euro once the rates are fixed on 1st January 1999

- Issuers recognise that there will be a huge and increasing pan-European investor base which will be insulated from currency risks once their currencies join EMU

- It is likely that there will less and less European government bonds in circulation both in total nominal value and in terms of proportion to the total value of bonds issued

- There is likely to be a growth in euro-denominated bond issuance by international and supranational issuers wanting to access the European investor base

- There is also likely to be massive growth in the issuance of corporate bonds.

Interest rates

- There is still vigorous debate as to which benchmark interest rate will become dominant for bonds and deposits, EURIBOR or EURO LIBOR. The important thing for practitioners is to know which one you are using. The following table sets out the differences and conventions:

	EURIBOR	EURO BBA LIBOR
Panel	57 banks: • 47 selected by national banking associations to represent the euro markets in the participating states • 10 international or pre-in banks active in the euro market with an office in the euro zone	16 major banks active in the euro market in London
Calculation basis	Discard top and bottom 15% and average remainder	Discard top and bottom 4 and average remainder
Time of fixing	11:00 Brussels time daily	11:00 London time daily
Fixing days	All days on which TARGET is in operation	All days on which TARGET is in operation
For value	Second TARGET day after rate fixing	Second TARGET day after rate fixing
Fixing periods	1 week, 1 month to 12 months	1 week, 1 month to 12 months

Courtesy of BBA - British Bankers Association

Derivatives

- As for euro denominated bond markets, euro derivatives have effectively already arrived

- The International Swap Dealers Association (ISDA) is promoting its ISDA EMU Protocol, which sets rules for making changes to existing ISDA master agreements governing swap trades

- This process is still evolving and there are some residual legal risks that are believed, however, to be quite small

- Counterparties should examine their current or potential derivatives contracts whether for swaps, options, futures and other structures to check, among other things, on contract continuity, successor floating rate indices - such as EURO LIBOR or EURIBOR and business day conventions

- It is important to recognise that while the market in euro related derivatives will become huge it is, as yet, in development phase.

Preparing for the future

Training and human resources

Many firms now have EMU working groups where they can share information and skills.

Larger firms in particular have found it both helpful and economical to pool resources in accounting, systems, pricing, treasury and other operations to ensure a co-ordinated approach and avoid duplicating work.

In most organisations, the finance and treasury areas are driving this. But it is not only a financial area. Many larger firms have already announced that they are shifting to Euro accounting as soon as possible and that they will expect their suppliers and business counterparties to be able to transact will them in euro.

Therefore, working groups should include representation across all disciplines of the business. Not least there is an important communication function to be performed.

Some firms are using regular memos, written briefings or newsletters as a means to keep their staff informed of EMU developments within and outside the firm. Others use e-mail or Intranets to ensure their staff are up to speed.

The nearer EMU gets, the more queries are likely to be raised by staff and customers. Some of the typical ones are listed in the FAQ section at the end of this booklet.

Giving advice to clients

EMU is usually perceived as a financial issue. Therefore, clients and customers will expect their banking, securities and financial services providers in general to play a leadership role.

While it very much depends what business and what aspect of that business you are concerned with, financial industry staff should expect to be able to answer frequently asked questions competently.

They should also have access points within their firms, where specialist staff conversant with the more complex or esoteric aspects of EMU, can be on hand to provide support in answering customer and client queries.

This requires careful planning and organisation. Many firms believe that providing good service and guidance on EMU issues will give them competitive advantages when it comes to gaining and retaining clients in the increasingly competitive pan–European financial services sector.

Legal implications

Contracts govern just about all forms of business activity. Some will be long, detailed and wordy, others will be deemed to exist, even if they are not formally written down.

There will be those which fall purely within the English or Scottish legal jurisdictions. These might include contracts of employment, property leases, contracts for provision of local services or contracts with UK–based clients. Others may be governed by other countries' legal codes.

Although the legal structures are now in place to ensure continuity of contracts following EMU, it is important to make some checks.

Check back over all existing contracts, particularly those involving other currencies, those which been in existence for some time or those involving foreign clients.

There may be provisions to review the contract's terms in the event of a requirement to change the currency of the contract.

It could be that the contract may only be

denominated in a particular currency. That currency may be set to disappear once EMU has been achieved.

It may mean preparing a formal amendment for signature by the parties to the contract. This may also be the opportunity to bring in new standard contracts and terms that will govern future business and include provisions to cover the move to a single currency when and if the UK joins.

It is important to review all contracts to be sure that they cover future business and that EMU and the eventual adoption the euro will not affect formal, contractual relations.

Accounting & systems changes

For most UK firms already accounting in foreign currencies, euro will be another – albeit important - currency.

It is likely to be sufficient to add euro to the list of currencies handled. Factor in the appropriate exchange rate to the system and deal with euro denominated business as you would with the French Franc, Deutschemark or other foreign currency accounting.

Businesses with operations in first round "in" countries will be able to operate in this way quite easily. One of the problems they may face however is that some of the tax, social security and other authorities in the some of the "in" countries will not be in a position to account in euros for quite some time. This may mean accounting in the local currency, euro and in Sterling where the operations are consolidated with the British parent company.

When and if Britain does join EMU, there will be a period of transition during which it will be necessary to run Sterling and euro accounts side-by-side. This may last some time but we cannot yet know how long.

One slight hitch at present is that computer keyboards do not carry a Euro symbol. However, nor do most standard UK ones carry any other symbol than Sterling and US Dollar. Eventually it is likely that keyboards will carry the euro symbol as standard.

Frequently Asked Questions

?

Q When will exchange rates against the euro be set?

A   Rates between the currencies of the "in" countries were set 3rd May 1998. See table on page 8. The value of the euro itself versus these currencies will be fixed on 31st December 1998.

Q Are "out" countries able to join if they are not part of the first round of participating states?

A   Yes. They need to apply to the European Council and achieve similar criteria to those achieved by the "in" countries.

Q What happens between when the exchange rates are fixed after 1999 but before the euro replaces national currencies in 2002?

A   Non-cash transactions can be conducted in euros from 1st January 1999. Cash transactions will be conducted in existing national currencies until euro replaces them.

Q Who will control interest rates after EMU?

A   Short term interest rates will be set centrally by the European Central Bank. Longer term ones will be determined by Member States.

Q What is the European Central Bank?

A   It is the central bank which will set monetary policy for all of the
11 participating Member States from 1st January 1999. Its
President will be Wim Duisenberg from Holland and Christian
Noyer of France will be Vice President.

**Q Will the European central banks still exist and where will the
Bank of England fit into the picture?**

A   The central banks of the European countries will still exist and they
will carry out the policy decisions set by the ECB. This system of
operation is called the European System of Central Banks (ESCB).

The Bank of England will not be a member of the ECB because the
UK will not be part of EMU. It will however have an advisory role.

**Q When will it be possible to open a euro denominated bank
account?**

A   By the start of EMU on 1st January 1999, a number of British and
European banks will be providing this service.

Q   What will the euro currency be like?

A   There will be 7 euro banknotes with the following denominations:
5, 10, 20, 50, 100, 200 and 500. There will be 8 Euro coins:
1,2,5,10,20,50 euro cents and 1 and 2 euros.

Q   Is there an alternative to the TARGET settlement system?

A   Not yet, but there will most likely be one in the future. A group of
banks is working on a project to transform the existing ECU
clearing system to a same day value system under the European
Banking Association.

Glossary

Amsterdam Summit

This took place in June 1997 and established the way euro and EU "out" country currencies will relate to each other.

Convergence

The process of aligning the economic performance of EMU member states prior to joining the single currency.

Conversion rates

The irrevocable fixed exchange rates at which currencies will convert to the euro.

ECB

European Central Bank - which is to be responsible for monetary policy including setting interest rates.

ECOFIN

Council of Finance Ministers of the European Union

Glossary

ECU

European Unit of Account. A so-called "basket currency" made up of the EU currencies. The forerunner of the euro used by the European Commission for accounting purposes and also for financial transactions such as bond issues and loans.

EMI

European Monetary Institute, based in Frankfurt, established on 1st January 1994 will be replaced by the ECB.

EMS

European Monetary System. A forerunner of EMU, it was aimed at improving monetary stability.

EMU

European Monetary Union - the process of locking together European economies currencies.

ERM

Exchange Rate Mechanism - a system of adjustable exchange rates used by members' countries whereby currencies operated within defined exchange rate bands.

ESCB

European System of Central Banks.

Glossary

Euro

The new currency to be used in the countries within the single market currency zone.

EURIBOR

A rate used for Euro interest rate fixings based upon dealings in the markets of Euro zone.

EURO LIBOR

A rate used for Euro interest rate fixings based upon dealings in the London market.

European Council

Made up of EU heads of state plus the President of the European Commission.

GDP

Gross domestic product.

Gilts / gilt edged stock / gilt edged securities

Bonds raised by the UK government to fund its activities.

"Ins"

The 11 EU countries which were included in the EMU area in the first round of membership. They are Austria, Belgium, Finland, France, Germany, Ireland, Italy, Luxembourg, Netherlands, Portugal and Spain.

Glossary

ISDA

The International Swap Dealers Association. This organisation has produced standard documentation to underpin derivative transactions.

Legacy currencies

The currencies of the member states participating in EMU. The legacy currencies will eventually disappear and be replaced by euro.

Maastricht Treaty

The Treaty on European Union which amended the Treaty of Rome. The Maastricht Treaty established key criteria which member countries needed to achieve in order to be eligible for EMU.

"Outs"

The 4 EU countries which were not included in the EMU area in the first round of membership. They are Denmark, Greece, Sweden and the UK.

TARGET

Trans-European Automated Real-Time Gross-Settlement Express Transfer - the wholesale same-day payment system for euros.

Transitional period

Beginning on 1st January 1999 and ending on 31st December 2001.

Useful Contacts

Bank of England
Public Enquiries Group (HO-1)
Threadneedle Street
London EC2R 8AH
0171 601 4878

Barclays Bank PLC
54 Lombard Street
London EC3P 3AH
0171 699 5000

British Bankers Association
Pinners Hall
105-108 Old Broad Street
London EC2N 1EX
0171 216 8800

British Retail Consortium
5 Grafton Street
London
W1X 3LB
0171 647 1500

Department of Trade and Industry

Europe Directorate

Kingsgate House

66-74 Victoria Street

London SW1E 6SW

0171 215 5000

European Commission

Refer to local EU information offices throughout
the country.

0171 973 1992

H.M. Treasury

Parliament Street

London SW1P 3AG

Public enquiry office

0171 270 4558

See also useful Web site at:

http://www.hm-treasury.gov.uk

National Westminster Bank

Corporate Banking Services

Level 11 Drapers Gardens

12 Throgmorton Avenue

London EC2N 2DL

Tel: 0171 920 1315

Publications

Economic & Monetary Union in Europe
Bank of England

Economic & Monetary Union
The European Commission, 1996
ISBN 92-827-5820-6, HMSO

The Single European Currency
A practical guide by The Hundred Group of
Finance Directors (March 1997) from KPMG
Distribution Centre
Tel: 01923 214807

Preparing for EMU - The implications of
European Monetary Union for the banking and
financial markets in the United Kingdom.
Report of the EMU City Working Group
(September 1996) from British Bankers
Association (see above)